*"The concept wor[ks...]
what it is that [...]
importantly, it give[s...]
method, to achiev[e...]*
Mark Ions, Managing Director, Exclusive Ltd.

Two Lengths

of

the Pool

Sometimes the simplest ideas have the greatest impact.

by
Simon Hartley

This edition first published 2013 by Be World Class

© 2013 Simon Hartley

Registered office
Be World Class Limited, Arkendale, North Yorkshire, HG5 0QU

For information about how to apply for permission to reuse the copyright material in this book, please contact caroline@be-world-class.com.

The right of the author to be identified as the author of this work has been asserted in accordance with the Copyright, Designs and Patents Act 1988.

All rights reserved. No part of this publication may be reproduced, stored in a retrieval system, or transmitted, in any form or by any means, electronic, mechanical, photocopying, recorded or otherwise, except as permitted by the UK Copyrights, Designs and Patents Act 1988, without the prior permission of the publisher.

Be World Class Limited publishes in a variety of print and electronic formats and by print-on-demand. Some material included with standard print versions of this book may not be included in other formats. Further information and material to support this book may be available at www.be-world-class.com

Designations used by companies and individuals to distinguish their products and services are often claimed as trademarks. All brand names and product names used in this book are trade names, service marks, trademarks and registered trademarks of their respective owners. The publisher is not associated with any product or vendor mentioned in this book, other than those of Be World Class Limited. This publication is designed to provide accurate and authoritative information in regard to the subject matter covered. It is sold on the basis that the publisher is not engaged in rendering professional services. If professional advice or other expert assistance is required, the services of a competent professional should be sought.

ISBN: 978-1484969854

Two Lengths of the Pool

Praise for Two Lengths of the Pool

"Clarity, Laser focused Clarity! That is probably the most important primary quality that Simon will inspire in you; he certainly has for me.

Without this laser focused clarity that Simon helps us to develop here, we simply create our very own human hamster wheel of activity that doesn't take us anywhere near where we want to go. Instead, it breeds frustration and a low self-image; generated by weak results from high levels of enthusiastic 'misdirected' effort.

The reason many of Simon's clients do succeed and do achieve outstanding world class results, is because they have the right influencer who helped them gain Clarity - laser focused Clarity of purpose. They know, understand and <u>own</u> their "2 lengths of the pool"

I am further inspired by watching Simon own his "2 Lengths of the pool" through our Challenge 2014".

Andy McMenemy, World-record breaking ultra-distance athlete and inspirational speaker.

"This book exemplifies Simons' unique ability to break down the complexities of life. His '2 Lengths' concept has dramatically changed my individual coaching program, and my life. It has enabled me to simplify my clients' process, and show them how to achieve greatness in their craft".

Greg Liberto, The HEAD Coach at Indaregolf.com

"Simon Hartley's newest book, "Two Lengths of the Pool" gives us a look at how a champion athlete's simplicity in task understanding helped him create the best process to succeed. It goes beyond wins and losses to the heart of what drives change- consistent and accumulated adjustments- and speaks to anyone with a job to do. Taking world-class athletic performance activities and transferring them into the business world is both useful and inspiring. This is a must read for anyone who is bogged down by distractions, endless to-do lists and organizational "noise".

Linda Wawrzyniak. Chair, Quality in Athletics. American Society for Quality.

Praise for Two Lengths of the Pool

"Five years ago I listened intently as a new, simple and innovative approach to developing teams and achieving success was delivered by Simon and Chris. 'Two Lengths of the Pool' was born and my desire to ensure that everyone within my business was on the same page, that everyone was aiming for the same goals and that everyone was achieving, ensured early adoption of the Two Lengths concept.

From experience I know that basic tick box appraisals will not achieve success. So what will? Simple – implementing, running and reviewing using the two lengths principles both personally and within your businesses.

The concept works – it allows you to focus on what is vital for your business, what it is that you are truly looking to achieve. More importantly, it gives you a powerful yet practical and simple method to achieving this.

Businesses fail due to a lack of clarity on direction, expectation and understanding.

Two Lengths allows you to define and refine your own personal business objectives; it allows your team to define and understand their own objectives and how these interlink to the businesses goals. Ultimately, it allows you total, quantifiable success for you and your business. A major achievement for any business owner."

Mark Ions, Founder and Managing Director of Exclusive Ltd – www.exclusiveltd.co.uk

Two Lengths of the Pool

Contents

Praise for Two Lengths of the Pool 5

Acknowledgements 10

Preface 11

Foreword, by Chris Cook 13

Why Read This Book? 16

Two Lengths of the Pool… What's it all about? 18

What's Your Two Lengths? 28

Your 5 Keys 47

Profiling Your Performance 57

Towards Mental Toughness 71

Case Study 83

Simple Does Not Always Mean Easy. 90

Summary 93

What's Next? 94

Bibliography and Useful Links 97

About Simon Hartley 100

Acknowledgements

I would like to say a huge thank you to everyone that has helped make this book possible.

Firstly, thank you very much, Chris Cook!

Thank you also to all of those who reviewed this book, gave their honest feedback and their endorsements. I am very grateful for them all.

Finally, thank you for reading it. I hope that you gain as much value from this very simple concept as we have.

I dedicate this book to my gorgeous wife and wonderful daughters.

Preface

For over 15 years, I have had the pleasure of working with elite athletes and sports teams. Some of these athletes and teams are amongst the very best in the world; world champions, world record breakers, top 5 world-ranked players, Olympians, gold medallists, and championship winning teams. As a sport psychology consultant, my job is to help them get their mental game right. Put simply, I help them to hone their focus, control their confidence, master their motivation, de-construct pressure and love their 'discomfort zone'.

Around eight years ago I was challenged to apply what I call 'sport psychology' to a sales team. The sales manager approached me and asked if I could help his team. It was the turn of the year and the team's target had increased by 50 per cent from the previous year. Interestingly, the team had only just scraped through in the previous year. The sales manager had a problem. He didn't believe the team could achieve the new target and neither did they. I'd never worked with a sales team before, so I decided to simply view the team as a group of athletes and apply my tried and tested sport psychology strategies. To my surprise, it worked extremely well. The team became confident, motivated and focused. As a result, they exceeded their targets.

Initially it took me a while to understand why it had worked so well. I was puzzled as to how sport psychology applied so easily to a business environment. The answer of course is very simple. There is a simple common denominator. We are all humans. Once I'd realized this, I began to apply the same principles to many other fields, including executive coaching, leadership and management development, performance management, other sales teams, education, healthcare and the charity sector.

I believe that the strategies that elite athletes and sports teams use can help us all to perform better, whatever our discipline. This book outlines one very simple concept that helped one athlete to become genuinely world class.

Foreword by Chris Cook

I have always believed that in order to achieve something worthwhile, you have to bring it into focus to be able to work towards it. I also believed that for a vast part of my swimming career I had that focus right, until one afternoon when I realised that we had an extremely complicated, uninspiring and meaningless focus.

Simon and I had one of our regular one-to-one sport psych sessions. I was feeling particularly flustered with the work load, the effects of physical training and the pressure of this seemingly enormous task; to achieve what I wanted from swimming. Simon sensed this and asked what was wrong. I explained that I had a lot on my plate in not so few words.

"That's strange', Simon replied, 'Surly your job is simply to swim 2 lengths of the pool as fast as you can".

I have to be honest; I wasn't best pleased with his comment at first. I felt as though he'd completely undermined and belittled my job. I mean, 'my job was pretty complicated' and 'he didn't understand what I had to do' and 'my role was much tougher than a simple phrase'... right? Or was it? These were all the things that surfaced in my mind as soon as we began to simplify what I was in sport to do. When I eventually came around to the idea, we discussed how we could simplify everything! Could we have a single focal point; to direct our attention towards the detail of our immense and intensely hard work... could it be done? And what would change if we committed to this? These were big questions that would have to be tackled head-on because I was beginning to realise that 'Simple doesn't always equate to easy', and it certainly wasn't in this case. We had to battle my ego, which was telling me that it had to be complicated. This was a big deal to me. It'd been my dream for as long as I could remember. We also had the challenge of potentially facing change.

The enormous impact the '2 lengths of the pool' focus had on my swimming career is something that still astounds me to this day. It not only made navigating my way towards my childhood dream crystal clear, but also assisted people in my team to understand where they fitted in and could maximise their impact upon my performance. Our team, and my performance, began to operate on a completely different level. We were now able to work on our true potential.

Chris Cook, Team GB Olympic Swimmer

Chris is a gold medal-winning 100m breaststroke swimmer. He was an Olympic finalist in Beijing 2008. He also won two Gold medals and a Silver medal at the Commonwealth Games in 2006. Chris held the Commonwealth record, he was a Bronze medallist in the World Championships in 2006 and Bronze medallist in the European Championships of 2004.

Chris finished his career as the 7th fastest man in history in his event and one of only a handful to swim the event in under 60 seconds.

For more information on Chris Cook, visit
www.chriscookgb.com
Twitter: @chriscookgb

Why Read This Book?

I am a great believer that the value in any information is realised when we use it. If you finish reading this book and say "it was interesting" or even "enjoyable", I don't think we will have achieved very much. If, on the other hand, you change and refine your approach in some way, it is likely that reading this book will be of great value.

This is not 'War and Peace'. It won't take you long to read from cover to cover. This is not a big book, and it doesn't have to be. The ideas are very simple. However, it can take a while to really understand the impact that these ideas can have on you and your performance. I've included some examples of how other people have applied these simple concepts to phenomenal effect. Although we can often pick up helpful tips from reading other people's experiences, it is far more important that you can adopt the principles in your own life.

I asked a friend of mine to review a draft of this book before it went to be published. He asked me why I'd written it, and what I wanted a reader to gain from it. It's a sensible question, I'm sure you'll agree. I told him that I wanted to help other people to be able to clarify and simplify their job, how to find their "2 Lengths" and "5 Keys", and how to extract the greatest possible benefit from them. I know how powerful this simple concept has been for the athletes, sports teams, executives and businesses that I've worked with. When they clarify and simplify, they become infinitely more effective and ultimately achieve more.

My hope is that, by reading this book, you can find your own "2 Lengths of the Pool" and the clarity that can transform your performance.

Two Lengths of the Pool... What's it all about?

It seems like a very strange phase doesn't it. You may well be thinking, "What do the words *Two Lengths of the Pool* mean, and how on earth does it relate to me and my performance?"

In truth, the *Two Lengths of the Pool* concept (or '2 Lengths' for short) is a very simple idea that I arrived at by accident, whilst working with a GB International Swimmer called Chris Cook. Although the concept first emerged in a high performance sporting environment I've found that, like many other areas of sport psychology, it applies to a wide variety of domains.

For many years, parallels have been drawn between sporting success and success in business. Sports coaches have been employed to help businesses develop a 'winning mentality'. There are numerous books on the market, which also aim to translate successful formulas from the world of sport into the commercial world. The question is; does it really work? Is there a direct and tangible benefit to the business? Could a business that is struggling in the current economic climate actually benefit from the experiences of elite athletes?

In 2010, Chris Cook and I started working with a Law Firm in the UK, to apply the "2 Lengths" concept to their business. They wanted to adopt the very strategies that helped Chris to win medals and break records. Since 2008, the commercial climate in the UK has become particularly tough for professional firms such as accountancy and legal firms. Noticeably, some well-established and well respected firms have gone out of business. This trend has made some leading firms sit up and take note. They realise that to survive and grow in this climate, they need to become smarter and more effective.

So... What Is The "2 Lengths" and Where Did It Come From?

Let's rewind to the beginning of the story.

In 2001, Chris was a decent National standard swimmer who had just competed at the World Student Games. He was ranked 32nd and had not yet won a full international cap. Between 2001 and around 2004-2005, we worked in a slight fog. Although Chris was making progress, the plan we were working to was a 'best guess'. It was a little bit reactionary. It almost felt like we were navigating in very poor visibility and reacting as things appeared. At the time Chris was working to a set of goals which included, 'making the GB team', 'securing funding', 'securing sponsorship', 'qualifying for championships' and 'winning key races'.

One afternoon, in around 2004-2005, Chris came into my office for one of our regular one-to-one sport psych sessions. He was looking particularly flustered. When I asked what was wrong,

Chris started to explain that he had a lot on his plate; correspondence with British Swimming regarding his funding, arranging travel to competitions, an awards dinner, training, etc. There is a technical term for this condition in sport psychology. Chris was 'a stress head'. After he'd finished, I said,

"That's strange. Surely your job is simply to swim 2 lengths of the pool as fast as you can".

I have to be honest; Chris didn't take too kindly to this at first. He felt as though I'd undermined and belittled his job. Initially, he thought, "my job is a bit more complicated than that, thank you very much". As he drove from my office at the English Institute of Sport back to the swimming pool, Chris paired my name with a number of choice expletives. As he says himself, his ego was hurting and it took a little while for him to get his head around the whole idea.

To hear him describing the experience in his own words, watch Chris Cook's session (entitled 'On... Talent') at www.beworldclass.tv

Until that point we had made a fundamental error. We got Chris' job wrong. His job was not to make the GB team. It wasn't to secure funding or sponsorship. It wasn't to qualify for championships or win races.

He was a 100m swimmer in a 50m pool. His job was very very simple. The job was to swim 2 lengths of the pool as quickly as he could.

What Impact Did This Have On Chris' Performance?

That realisation was like a blinding flash of light. It made an enormous impact on how he worked, his effectiveness and the end results. Immediately he started to identify *exactly* what he needed to do in order to swim 2 lengths of the pool as quickly as he could. He pulled together his team of specialists, which included his coach, physiotherapist, performance analyst, nutritionist, physiologist, strength & conditioning coach, performance lifestyle advisor and me. Everyone was challenged to help him swim 2 lengths of the pool as quickly as he possibly could. His whole outlook changed once he figured out what his real job was.

It became a benchmark and a filter. Before doing anything, Chris would ask "will this help me swim 2 lengths of the pool quicker?" He challenged his team whenever he walked into a training session by asking, "How will this session help me to swim 2 lengths of the pool quicker?" As he walked into each and every training session or competition, Chris knew exactly how it was going to contribute to his performance.

If there was a method, strategy, practice or technique that would make him quicker, he'd consider doing it. If not, it would be rejected. We also started asking whether it was likely to knock a whole second off of his time or 0.000001 seconds. Obviously, the things which made a bigger impact had a higher priority. Chris actually identified the 5 key processes that he required. These were the processes which had the greatest positive impact on his performance.

Once he had identified these, he focused his time and energies into delivering these key processes.

We Broke All The Rules That Never Existed

Of course, the 'rules' were never rules. They were conventions. Rather than perpetuating the habits that had governed his training programme for the last few years, we questioned it and challenged it. Were all of these sessions actually contributing? Were they helping Chris swim quicker? We turned the whole approach on its head and started by looking at how we could make him quicker. Interestingly, Bradley Wiggins (2012) describes going through a similar process with his sport scientist, Tim Kerrison, in his book *My Time*.

We broke down Chris' stroke. We analysed his technique. He started to figure out what the key elements of his performance were and put programmes in place to improve them. He changed his training regime to take out many of the things he had habitually done (because they had always been on the programme) and replaced them with things that would contribute to swimming 2 lengths quicker.

Two Lengths of the Pool...What's it all about?

We identified that Chris needed to flatten the angle at his hips to reduce his drag in the water. Out went some of the swim sessions and strength sessions that were not really contributing. In came yoga, gymnastics and specialist physiotherapy work to improve his streamlining. We also found that he needed more strength in the very first part of his arm movement (the phase of his stroke when his arms were stretched out in front of him). To do this he used gymnastics rings and a climbing wall instead of dumb-bells and weights.

We spent two to three years working on a project to help improve his starts by a few tenths of a second, and another to work on his turns. Chris did some of the sessions in a gymnastics hall, diving into a pit full of foam bricks, rather than a pool full of water. We analysed his performances to find the perfect race strategy for him and then put a programme in place to practice this and perfect it. Chris even found a new warm up for competitions. Rather than ploughing up and down swimming lengths with the others, Chris would often sit or lie on the bottom of the pool and simply attune himself with the water.

Interestingly, when he looked back, Chris noticed that he had ditched 60 per cent of his training programme. He questioned whether he needed to swim tens of thousands of meters in the pool every week. When we looked at it honestly and objectively, it became obvious that he had adopted his training programme out of habit, not because it was the most effective possible.

This thought process set up our working practice for the last four or five years of his career. It helped Chris to become infinitely more focused, more effective and more successful. The results were dramatic. Because he could swim 2 lengths of the pool more quickly, he won more races, became a regular on the British team (and in fact became British and Commonwealth number one for several years), he qualified for major championships, made finals at World Championships, and Olympic Games, and won two gold medals at the Commonwealth Games. The final race of Chris' career was an Olympic Final in Beijing 2008 and he ended his career as the 7th fastest 100m breaststroke swimmer in history.

Does This Really Apply To Me?
Many individuals and organisations are now using exactly the same principles to enhance their effectiveness, including the UK law firm that I mentioned earlier. They have found their own '2 Lengths of the Pool'. This is not a mission statement or a vision. Instead, it is a statement of their job in the simplest possible terms. It provides them with the clarity and simplicity that gives them complete focus. The senior partners have also agreed upon the most important processes required to achieve their '2 Lengths' successfully. As a result, they can cascade this clear focus throughout the business. They can also establish their own filters and benchmark their effectiveness. To ensure that this new way of working starts to live and breathe, and become part of the culture, it has also become embedded in the performance management structures.

Everyone's job is aligned to the '2 Lengths' for the firm and the processes which are required to achieve it. As a result, every member of the team has a clear focus, which is completely aligned to achieving the '2 Lengths' of the firm.

Obviously, the process doesn't happen overnight. The project with the Law Firm spanned over nine months and included several reviews along the way. Results from the early stages of the project show that the effectiveness of the senior management team has increased significantly. The partners realise that, before the project, there was a significant amount of time spent on 'garbage'. The 'garbage' (aka distractions from their core job) was reducing their effectiveness. The Managing Partner of the firm actually told me that they have binned 60 per cent of what they were doing because it was not contributing to their 2 Lengths.

Hang on... 60 per cent... haven't we heard that somewhere before?

Pressure… What Pressure?

As well as helping to focus Chris' training, we also found that the '2 Lengths of the Pool' concept helped to reduce his perception of 'pressure' during competition. Here's an excerpt from an article that I wrote, entitled *'Pressure… What Pressure?'* The full article, and accompanying webinar, is available at www.be-world-class.com.

Athletes feel 'pressure' when they get *the job* wrong. Typically athletes think that their job is to win, to climb up the rankings, to secure prize money or sponsorship. However, none of those things are *the job*. Normally when we get the job wrong, it is because we're too busy focusing on the outcome. In reality, our job is to deliver the process. By aiming for the result, we set ourselves a job which is outside of our control. The fact that it is outside of our control means that it's uncertain. Winning is never certain. Hitting a target is never certain. There is always an element of uncertainty. This uncertainty is what tends to cause us the angst. How can we be completely confident in our ability to achieve something that has uncertainty? If you're trying to do an 'impossible' job or even a job which you have no control over, you will probably imagine pressure because you will not be 100 per cent sure that you can do the job. The job might seem too big or too daunting. If the athlete believes the job is to win the tournament, they might doubt their ability to do it. Even a confident athlete won't *know* that they can do that job. There is often a gap between what we believe we can achieve, and what we think we must achieve. That gap manifests as the worry and anxiety we associate with pressure. This is illustrated in the model of the Challenge and Skills Balance (found on page 46 of *Peak Performance Every Time*, published in 2011 by Routledge). If we create an expectation for ourselves (or take on board someone else's expectations), we post a target. If we are not absolutely sure that we can achieve that target, we might start to have doubts and worries. If we also give that target some meaning, we will magnify our doubts and worries.

As we've said already, we create pressure therefore we can 'de-construct it'. The easiest way is not to create it in the first place. However, if we do feel pressure, we have the ability to dismantle it and start to see the reality rather than the illusion. If you start to perceive pressure, take a few moments to remind yourself why there is no pressure and never was any pressure. Normally this involves a slight reality check and a quick reminder of *the job*. Once we do that, we are more likely to be able to focus on exactly what we need to do in that moment. In reality the job we need to do will normally be pretty simple and something we're very capable of doing. Rather than trying to 'serve for the match' or 'win Championship point', we'll simply be trying to serve. Instead of trying to win the World Cup, the job is simply to take a penalty kick. Rather than attempting to win the Ryder Cup, the job is simply to execute a 3 foot putt.

Chris knew that his only job was to swim 2 Lengths of the Pool as fast as he could. This didn't change, regardless of whether he was in a training session or an Olympic Final.

What's Your Two Lengths?

So, how do you find your own 2 Lengths of the Pool? What is your job in the simplest possible terms? To start the thought process, let's take a look at Chris' job again in more detail. His job was...

To swim – not run, walk, kayak or row.
Two lengths of the pool – not one, three, four, six or eight.
As fast – because his criterion measure is speed (time), not profit, height or distance jumped.
As I can – not as fast as someone else can. Chris' aim was not to win. His aim was not to swim his 2 lengths in under 60 seconds.

Many athletes, coaches and business leaders that I work with can appreciate the first three parts of this quartet but struggle with the fourth. I've heard so many people say, "well surely he wanted to win" and "he must have had a goal to hit a certain time". The answer to both of those comments is, "yes, but that doesn't change his 2 lengths statement".

All athletes want to win. However, Chris' job was not to beat the guys next to him. The simple truth is that if Chris swam as fast as he could, and someone else swam quicker, they would win. If he swam as fast as he could, and nobody swam quicker, he'd win. That's it. It really doesn't get any more complicated than that.

Equally, if the fastest he could possibly swim was 60.1 seconds, why would we say "under 60 seconds"? If the fastest he could possibly swim was 58.7 second, why would we say "under 60 seconds" rather than "under 59 seconds"? The aim was always to swim as fast as possible. I am currently preparing to embark on an endurance challenge in aid of three charities (we've called it Challenge 2014). It's a 40 day challenge that will take us around Great Britain. I've been asked how much money we're aiming to raise. The answer is "as much money as we possibly can". The response from most people is, "yes, but how many pounds?" My answer is, "as many as we possibly can". There is no other answer. Why would there be a different answer?

Chris' '2 Lengths' statement is complete. When he achieves it, he will have done everything necessary to be successful. In his terms, 'success' meant achieving his potential and being the best that he could be. As we said, his criterion measure is speed. He wasn't interested in having the best technique, being the most attractive swimmer or making the most money from his swimming career. In business, arguably the '2 Lengths' needs to contain an element of profitability; it is part of the criterion measure in commerce. If a company has a '2 Lengths' that ignored profit, there is a chance that it could deliver its '2 Lengths' but go out of business.

Critically, Chris Cook's 2 Lengths of the Pool is composed of processes, not outcomes. This is a fundamental part of what made it so powerful.

Processes & Focus

When we focus on the processes, we stand a much better chance of delivering them. When we deliver the processes consistently well, we stand a much better chance of being successful. If you focus on delivering a '2 Lengths' that is based on processes, you'll be able to direct your efforts far more effectively.

Processes & Confidence

I often talk to athletes about their confidence in the lead up to competitions. If I asked them how confident they are in delivering their processes, most will tell me that they're very confident. If I asked them how confident they were in winning, they'll be less confident. By focusing on processes, we also focus our attention onto things that we have more control over. Generally, the outcome is not something that is within our control. There are normally a host of variables that affect the outcome, whether it is the result in sport or hitting a sales target in business. However, the processes often are within our control. Improving our ability to execute the processes is also something that we have control over. Many people spend too much time worrying about the outcome, rather than focusing on delivering the processes.

Processes & Motivation

A lot of people become disillusioned and demotivated if they set a goal or a target and don't achieve it. If we said that the fund-raising target for Challenge 2014 is £1,000,000 and we raise £999,999, we've failed. If we only raise £300,000 we're likely to feel pretty disappointed. If the target is £1,000,000 and we've been working extremely hard to raise just £100,000, we're likely to give up on our big target because we'll see it as impossible.

Often our judgment of 'success' or 'failure' is based on our expectations. If we expect to achieve X and we fall short in some way, we judge that we've failed and often become demotivated. If we exceed X, we feel like we've succeeded. That sounds pretty logical doesn't it? However, it's actually a very fragile system, especially when X is an outcome over which we have limited influence. The expectation (the X) is normally arbitrary too. It's an idea... a projection into the future. It is a product of our imagination (as all projections and visions of the future are) and is therefore a 'fantasy'.

If we swapped our outcome based 'goals' and 'targets' for a '2 Lengths' that is based on processes that we have more control over, we are likely to have far more stable focus, confidence and motivation.

The Power of Synchronicity

A few years ago I took part in a CPD (Continual Professional Development) day with the English Institute of Sport. It is always beneficial for practitioners to understand the athletes' experiences. On this particular day, we (the team of sport psychologists, physiotherapists, strength & conditioning coaches, performance analysts, bio-mechanists and physiologists) were taken to the rowing club and thrown into some boats. I'm 6 feet tall and a former rugby player. I'm relatively strong and well built, so I thought that rowing might suit me quite well. Towards the end of the day it was time to put our experiences into practice and race each other. We were put into pairs and given a 2-man boat. I was paired with one of the strength and conditioning coaches, Tom. He was a pretty similar build to me, so we thought we had a decent chance. We found ourselves pitched in a head to head against our physiotherapist and bio-mechanist. Both girls were about 2 feet tall and about an inch wide. They weighed in at around 4 oz wet through. Tom and I started to think that we had this race in the bag.

I learnt a very powerful lesson that day. Tom and I pulled for all we were worth, but the boat hardly moved. We heaved and we grunted. We put in enormous effort, but struggled to generate any speed because we didn't manage to synchronise our strokes. Across the water, the two girls synchronised perfectly, and their boat sped off up the river. Occasionally Tom and I managed to get our blades into the water at the same time and the boat surged. Then we'd miss a few and lose the momentum. Of course, we were soundly beaten. Tom and I got out of the boat exhausted. We had put in an enormous amount of effort but, because we weren't synchronised, a lot of it was wasted.

I don't remember much from my Maths lessons at school. However, I do recall my teacher talking to us about vectors. A vector quantity is, as I remember it, composed not just of size but also direction. If you add a number of vectors together, you can see the overall distance travelled. For example...

If you add 3 meters, plus 4 meters, plus 3 meters, you'd expect to get 10 meters. However, if the three distances are all taken in different directions, you could get a lot less.

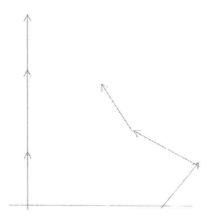

Imagine that these lines don't depict meters. Imagine that they illustrate the efforts of your team. Are you synchronised? Are you all pulling in the same direction? Where are your vectors taking you? Are you going where you want to go, or are you heading off course? How much of that energy is actually propelling you forwards, and how much is being directed sideways, or even backwards?

The irony is that if we were synchronised, Tom and I could have put a lot less effort in and made the boat move a lot quicker.

Alignment.

As you begin to identify your 2 Lengths of the Pool, it is important to understand how it fits with others. For example, if you are in business I would ask how your 2 Lengths fits into that of the business. I work closely with a number of organisations, both in sport and outside of sport, to help them achieve alignment.

The principle is very simple. What is the 2 Lengths of the Pool for the organisation? What is its job in the simplest possible terms? How does your 2 Lengths of the Pool contribute to that of the organisation? There should be a clear link between them.

This thought process applies equally to large organisations and small, sports teams and corporate businesses. Each player in a soccer team should know their own '2 Lengths' (based on their individual role and position) and how it contributes to that of the team. I believe that the '2 Lengths' for a soccer team is very simple. I don't believe that the aim of the game is to win (I can see coaches around the world jumping up and down in disagreement already). I believe the '2 Lengths' for a soccer team is...

"To score as many goals as possible and concede as few as possible".

Two Lengths of the Pool

Okay, STOP! Did I read that right? You just said the job was not to win, but to score as many goals as possible and concede as few. What's the difference?

Let me give you an example from an English soccer team that I worked with recently. The team manager called me in to do some sport psych work with the squad because they were starting games well but losing their lead. Sometimes they would go two to three goals up and then start to lose their way. The manager couldn't understand what was going on. I met with the team and asked them what they thought their "2 Lengths" was. Initially, they said that it was to win. I believe that's where the problem lay. If they think that the job is to win, it is likely that they'll take their foot off the gas if they feel that the job is already done. However, if the job is to score as many goals as possible, and concede as few as possible, they should still do that even if they are 3-0 up after 20 minutes. If they could score a fourth, they should. If they could stop their opponents scoring, they should. I'd argue that it is not good enough to win the game by one goal, if you could win by two or more. The job remains the same no matter what the score is, or how far through the game they are. By focusing on scoring as many as possible and conceding as few, they remained focused on the key processes for the entire game. As a result, they began to maintain and extend their lead in the game, rather than lose it. No doubt you'll see how this principle translates to sales targets and other outcome goals.

When a soccer team aims to score as many as possible, and concede as few as possible, it stands a much better chance of winning the game. Within the team, each individual can align their personal '2 Lengths' to make sure it contributes to scoring as many goals as possible and conceding as few as possible. Some players are more focused on scoring and others on preventing the opposition from scoring. It's similar in business. Some people will be focused on increasing income and others on minimising expenses. However, arguably, all the players in the soccer team should be focused on those two elements.

In larger organisations, there could be other layers. For example, the company will have its '2 Lengths'. Within that, there will be departments and teams. Each will have a '2 Lengths' that contributes to the company. The individuals within the teams will have their personal '2 Lengths' that is aligned to the team and therefore to the company. When I go through this exercise within organisations there are normally some very interesting findings.

The Range of Perceptions.

I asked a senior management team of over 30 people what the '2 Lengths of the Pool' was for the organisation. The range of different answers from the group was quite astounding, given that they were all leading the same organisation. There was a great deal of discussion as to their job (what they did and didn't do as a business). The team also debated whether 'profit' should feature or not. I suppose that finding a range of perspectives is not surprising when you take a group of over 30 people. However, I have also found significant differences of opinion when working with a board room team of two directors, who had very different views as to the job of their business.

"Do we all have a common view of this organisation?"

When we ask questions like, "does this project fit with our organisation?" and "is this the right strategy for us?" we need to have a common view on our '2 Lengths'.

My Perception vs Yours

One day I asked a manager and a team member to independently write down their version of the team member's personal '2 Lengths'. It became obvious very quickly that the team member's view and the manager's view were quite different. Having done the exercise a number of times now, I've found that misalignments, between the manager's view and that of the team member, to be commonplace. I've seen sports coaches shouting at players for not 'doing their jobs' on the field. When you talk to them independently, their perceptions of 'the job' are very different. However, each of them assumes that the other party perceives it the same way they do.

Gaps and Overlaps

Once you have identified the '2 Lengths' for the individuals and teams within an organisation, it's possible to see whether the summation of the parts actually delivers the whole. If everyone delivers their '2 Lengths', will the organisation deliver its '2 Lengths'? Are there any gaps? Are there significant overlaps? When working with a highly specialised engineering business, we found that nobody was responsible for protecting the Intellectual Property (patenting of designs, etc), even though it was strategically important to them.

Ownership and Responsibility

In addition to the gaps and overlaps, it is also possible to identify lines of ownership and responsibility. The '2 Lengths' help to show who should be taking ownership and have responsibility. Sometimes there is a difference between 'who does' and 'who should' be taking ownership.

Within a manufacturing business, we discovered that one of the most important areas of the company's strategy was not being picked up by anyone. Their strategy was based on delivering products into 'niche markets'. Therefore, 'identifying niche markets' was crucial to their success. Although it was clear which department was responsible, none of the individuals within that department included this element within their personal '2 Lengths'. When we discussed the issue, it was also apparent that none of them had the skills or confidence to take on the challenge.

Inter-dependency

When we pull all of the personal and departmental '2 Lengths' together for an organisation, we also start to see the lines of inter-dependency. Inevitably, within an organisation, people and teams rely on each other. Each person needs others to provide them with information and support in order to do their job. Everyone depends on others and, in turn, have people that are dependent upon them.

"I need you to do X for me, so that I can do Y"

Once these lines of inter-dependency are drawn, each person and team can see how they contribute to the whole.

Focus = Power

Clarity and focus are incredibly powerful. Many people find that they procrastinate because they do not have a simple, clear focus. A lack of clarity can make challenges seem daunting. If a task looks too big and we don't know where, or how, to start we can find ourselves rooted to the spot; unable to get going. Clarity is often the catalyst that gets us moving.

Simply knowing how we contribute, and why our role is important, often provides us with a great deal of motivation. Many people find that just knowing their '2 Lengths', and how it contributes to that of the organisation, increases their level of motivation and engagement. Clarity also helps them to refine what they do, ditch those things that don't contribute, and direct their energies more effectively. When we do this we tend to perform better. When we perform better we tend to become more confident, enjoy what we're doing, and want to do it again.

There is more information on the relationship between focus, confidence and motivation, in Chapter 2 of *Peak Performance Every Time*.

So... What's Your '2 Lengths'?

It's normally easy to see someone else's '2 Lengths of the Pool', but a lot harder to distil our own. Before focusing on finding your own, have a look at some examples from other individuals and organisations.

- A Long Jumper – '*To jump as far as possible into the sand-pit*'.
- A Javelin Thrower – '*To throw the javelin as far down the field as possible*'.
- A Professional Tour Golfer – '*To get the little white ball into the little hole in as few shots as possible*'

- A Recruitment and HR Consultancy Business – *'Deliver exceptional professional recruitment and HR consultancy services, profitably'*.
- A Development Forum For Business Owners & Leaders – *'Profitably provide the most challenging forums and 1-2-1 coaching we can'*.
- A Specialist Engineering Business – *'To deliver into niche markets, the best and most appropriate products and services, ethically and profitably'*.

You'll notice that like Chris Cook's '2 Lengths', these are complete statements. They are based on processes, not outcomes. Therefore, they encapsulate what the person or organisation does, not just what it wants to achieve. None of these statements talk of turnover or sales targets, medals, records or championships. However, when these people and organisations deliver their '2 Lengths', they will give themselves the best possible chance of being successful.

There are more examples from business and sport on page 36 of *Peak Performance Every Time*.

With all of these examples in mind, have a think about the "2 Lengths" for these people…

An Olympic Archer
- Each archer shoots 72 arrows in a competition.
- Each arrow scores points, depending on where it lands.

- The highest score is achieved by hitting the 'gold' in the centre of the target. The outer-most ring receives the least number of points.
- The winner is the archer with the most points after 72 arrows.

The Chief Executive Officer (CEO) of Widgets Ltd.
- The CEO is 'the boss' of the business.
- The company makes and sells 'widgets'.

The Sales Executive at Widgets Ltd.
- The Sales Executive is employed by Widgets Ltd to sell their 'widgets'.

You'll have some ideas on the '2 Lengths' for our three examples. There are no right or wrong answers, but here's what we came up with.

Olympic Archer

'To shoot 72 arrows as close to the centre of the target as possible'.

The CEO

'To ensure that the business delivers its 2 Lengths of the Pool'

The Sales Executive

'To sell as many widgets as possible'

Having worked with a number of different business organisations, I have seen a wide range of '2 Lengths'. Invariably the '2 Lengths' for CEOs and MDs from different businesses will vary, as will Sales Executives, HR Directors, Finance Directors and administrators. For example a sales executive may, or may not, have direct influence over the level of profit in the product they sell. Some will determine the price that they sell their products (and therefore the margin) and others will not. There are some sales executives who are targeted purely on the volume of products that they sell. Therefore some of the '2 Lengths' for sales executives include the words 'with the greatest possible margin' and some do not. One insurance salesman describes his '2 Lengths' in the following way...

"To generate as many high quality leads as possible and convert as many as I can into repeating sales".

It's a little more 'wordy', but really helped him to focus on those things that would make him successful.

Over To You!

It's your turn now. How would you describe your '2 Lengths'? What do you do, in the simplest possible terms?

Have a go at a first draft. It doesn't have to be perfect. As my Ph.D. tutor said to me, 'Don't wait until you have the perfect opening line before you start writing. Write something... anything... because you can always edit it later'.

My "2 Lengths"

_____

_____

Here's a quick checklist to help you know whether you're on the right course.

1. It needs to be a process, not an outcome.
2. It has to be entirely within your control.
3. It should fit neatly behind the words... "My / Our job is to..."
4. It needs to be very specific.
5. We need to know that if we achieve the 2 Lengths, we've accomplished the job completely and given ourselves the greatest chance of being successful.

Let's take a quick look at Chris' "2 Lengths of the Pool" and run it through the checklist.

It was process based and was entirely within his control. Chris knew that he was not always going to swim a personal best (p.b.). If he was in the middle of heavy training, his fastest swim could be a few per cent slower than his personal best. The job was not to swim a p.b., it was to swim as fast as he could.

Two Lengths of the Pool

It fitted neatly behind the words 'My job is.... *to swim 2 lengths of the pool as fast as I can*'

It was also very specific. It was to *swim* (not travel), *2 lengths* (a very specific distance).

When Chris delivered his '2 Lengths' the international caps, medals, records, sponsorship offers and funding all followed.

Do you need (or want) to edit your original '2 Lengths' after having run it through the checklist?

Once you have your '2 Lengths' you may find that it helps you to clarify your messages to others. The 'elevator pitch' is a classic example. I have heard many people attempt to deliver an 'elevator pitch'; that 30 second description of what you do and why it has value. Many people struggle to summarise what they do and the value of it into a 30 second pitch. It must be like trying to stuff everything you need for your two week holiday into an overnight bag. However, if you have a clear '2 Lengths', the challenge changes in your favour. Rather than thinking about what you're going to leave out, you can start with a very concise statement and focus on what to add to it.

Your
5 Keys

Simply knowing your 2 Lengths can provide a great deal of clarity. However, it is only half of the picture. Once we understood that Chris' job was to swim 2 lengths of the pool as quickly as he could, the next question was… "*How* do we do that?"

The '2 Lengths' give us 'the *what*'

The 5 Keys give us 'the *how*'

I asked Chris, "What are the 5 most important, most significant things that you need to do in order to swim 2 lengths of the pool as fast as you can? Which 5 things will have the greatest impact on your performance? You're only allowed 5, so make sure that you give me the most crucial, most vital things'.

Why 5?

Have you heard the saying 'Less is more'? I believe that there is often a lot of wisdom in that saying. Before Chris and I stumbled across the '2 Lengths of the Pool' idea, he fell into the trap that many people fall into. Chris was a very professional athlete (one of the best that I've worked with), which of course meant that he was very dedicated and diligent. If you asked Chris to write down all the things he could do to become quicker, he'd write a list of several hundred things. Like many professional and diligent people, Chris would try to do all of the several hundred things. He'd end up spreading himself too thinly by trying to do all of them. He wouldn't see any great return on the energy that he was expending and would often get frustrated. Like many other people, he worked extremely hard but didn't feel as if he was getting a fair return for his efforts.

I remember speaking to a head coach of one of our Great Britain Olympic squads when they returned home after the Beijing Games in 2008. He and his squad were disappointed because they'd come back without a medal. I asked the coach to tell me the 5 most important things that each of his athletes should focus on when performing. He said that it was impossible to narrow it down to just 5. When we discussed it further, the coach outlined 32 vital processes that the athletes needed to focus on when they performed. All of a sudden I realised why the squad had struggled in Beijing. I suspect that even the greatest mind on Earth would find it tough to focus on 32 things during their performance.

The 5 Keys are a way of simplifying and clarifying the most significant processes; those that have the greatest impact on our performance. I often describe them by saying, "if you deliver these 5 things, you're almost guaranteed to deliver your 2 Lengths".

Chris started to understand how much impact various elements actually had on his swimming speed. We used a very technical term, known as "the big chunks". We'd ask if a particular technique, method or idea would knock a 'big chunk' off of his time (i.e. a second, or half a second), or whether it was going to shave a fraction of a nano-second from his performance. Those things that made the greatest contribution received the greatest attention. For example, Chris worked for many years on his start (the time that elapsed between the 'starting gun' and Chris reaching the 15 meter mark). We worked for many years to knock 0.3 seconds off of this start time because it was one of his 5 Keys.

To help him swim 2 lengths of the pool as fast as he could, Chris' 5 Keys were...

1. Fast Start
2. Fast, but efficient, first length (which we referred to as 'easy speed')
3. Fast turn and exit
4. Hold the stroke and speed for as long as possible during the second length
5. Touch the wall with 2 hands

There are lots of different components that are required within each of these keys. For example, the first four keys require Chris to be as streamlined as possible. Therefore, we invested a lot of time, effort, energy, thought and attention to flattening the angle at Chris' hips. It lead us to drop some of the swimming sessions in favour of yoga and stretching work. On one occasion Chris dived into the pool during one of his 'starts' sessions. As he swam back to the side of the pool I asked him, "how did that feel?" He said, "My big toe was sticking out slightly and I could feel the drag coming off of it, so I'll need to tuck that in more". It shows that Chris understood how all the tiny details fitted into the 5 Keys and into his 2 Lengths.

How Does This Apply Beyond Swimming?

It sounds reasonable to think that swimming 2 lengths of a swimming pool can be honed down to just 5 keys. Can the same thought process really apply to an organisation or a business?

Here are some examples from some other individuals and organisations. These are not a generic set of keys that will be applicable to other operators in their disciplines. These keys work because they are personal and suited to the context of those that gave birth to them. As you'll see, the keys are presented in the words of those to whom they belong.

A Professional Tour Golfer

2 Lengths: "To get the little white ball into the little hole in as few shots as possible"

5 Keys:

1. Prepare well – body, mind, emotions and equipment.
2. Select the most appropriate shot (take each shot on its own merit).
3. Play each shot individually and on its own merit.
4. Consistently execute shots well – reliably (predictably) & accurately.
5. Learn from everything (mistakes are opportunities to learn).

An Elite Sports Team

2 Lengths: "*To score as many goals as possible and concede as few as possible*"

5 Keys:

1. Create as many shooting opportunities as possible when we regain possession
2. Convert as many shooting opportunities into goals as possible
3. Minimise the number of opposition shooting opportunities when we lose possession
4. Compete at high intensity for the entire game, including any extra-time.
5. Every player – be the best that you can be at all times.

A Recruitment & HR Consultancy Business

2 Lengths: *"Deliver exceptional professional recruitment and HR consultancy services, profitably"*

5 Keys:

1. Strong pipeline of high quality leads and live vacancies.
2. Strong candidates that are right for the vacancies.
3. Right product, service and price for the market.
4. A strong team – the right people performing at their best.
5. High quality management information, processes, checks and balances.

A Specialist Engineering Business

2 Lengths: *'To deliver into niche markets the best and most appropriate products and services, ethically and profitably'*.

5 Keys:

1. Identify the needs of niche markets.
2. Consistently develop (design), market & sell our products and services into niche markets.
3. Deliver (manufacture) our products & services reliably and consistently.
4. Be profitable, whilst upholding our ethical values and sustainability.
5. Continually improve what we do (highest impact areas first).

The 5 Keys Are Not…

These 5 Keys should not be simply a statement of what you currently do. Some people struggle to find their 5 Keys because they attempt to squash everything they do into 5 bullet points. That is not the aim of the exercise. If we did that, we'd end up achieving very little. The point of the exercise is to understand the 5 most significant elements that contribute to delivering your 2 Lengths. In reality, many people dedicate very little time, energy and focus to their 5 Keys because they are tied up with distractions.

Where Do We Start?

It's often good to begin by brainstorming what you do and identifying those things that really do make a significant contribution to your 2 Lengths. You may start to see some patterns emerging and common threads appearing. For example, we may have a multitude of different tasks that we need to do. If we tried to list the tasks as our Keys, we will never narrow it down to just 5. However, within each task there may be some common elements. One of my clients had this challenge. Within a manufacturing business there is one department that has responsibility for a very wide range of functions, from finance to HR, quality management, and health & safety. Finding the 5 Keys for this particular department looks like an almost impossible task at first glance. However, within each function there are aspects that they need to deliver. One such example is the production of accurate and timely management information, which then becomes one of their Keys.

The Devil (And Angels) Are All In The Detail.

The words that we use to define the Keys are very important. You may have noticed that the 5 Keys for the Professional Tour Golfer (above) contain words such as 'select the most appropriate shot' and 'execute the shot'. When we started the conversation, the words the player used were quite vague. Initially, he used phrases like 'play the best shot'. However, when we discussed it in more detail, we found that to 'play the best shot' he needed to select the most appropriate shot and then execute it well. When I asked what executing 'well' actually meant, he described shots that were consistently accurate and reliable (predictable).

To get beyond some of the vagueness, I'll often ask people what they mean by that term. You'll spot some of these terms in the 5 Keys presented above. There are some usual suspects, such as 'effectively', 'right', 'best' and 'well'. Often I don't know what 'effectively' means because I don't know the industry. An Operations Director once told me that they wanted to run an 'effective manufacturing operation'. I didn't know what an effective manufacturing unit looked like, because I have no background in it. So I asked, "How would I know an effective manufacturing unit? What would I see? If we lined up 5 manufacturing units, which varied in quality from 'world class' to 'diabolical', how would I spot the best ones?"

This naivety is actually very powerful for me. It helps me to ask the 'stupid questions', which bring us closer to a clear answer. As the Operations Director began to explain the differences, we were able to distil the key features that distinguished the better units, and therefore understand what 'effective' meant. If I understand 'effective' in the same way as the Ops Director there is a much greater chance that those within the Ops Team, and the rest of the business, will also understand it in the same way. If 'effective' means something different to everyone, we are likely to have a problem!

I have also noticed that people often use words that have very different meanings, interchangeably. In particular, there are the 'E' words, such as 'ensure', 'enable' and 'encourage'. There is a significant difference in the level of responsibility that comes with these three words. Ensure, indicates that it is our responsibility to make sure it happens. Enable, indicates that we are going to take responsibility for providing people with the tools, skills and resources to deliver. Encourage suggests that we'll try to support them in their endeavours. I am a great believer in making sure that the words we use are the ones we mean. Sometimes it is worth spending the time to scrutinise your 5 Keys in this way.

The Stress Test

I am a great fan of stress testing the 5 Keys for a couple of weeks. Once you've decided upon them, take some time to find out whether they really are the most significant and impactful elements. I often suggest that people press the 'pause' button on their day and review the previous few hours. Have you been focused on delivering your 5 Keys, or have you been doing something entirely different? If you find that your morning has been spent doing something distinctly different than your 5 Keys, it is time to ask some questions.

Are my 5 Keys right and my morning has been filled with distractions?

Or...

Do I need to change my 5 Keys because there is an important element that I missed out?

It is also worth taking a few minutes to compare how much of your overall time, focus, energy and resource you currently invest into each of the 5 Keys, to the amount you think is optimal. It's a good way to identify whether there are any mismatches anywhere, or if there are any Keys that don't get the focus they deserve.

Profiling Your Performance

Simply having a '2 Lengths of the Pool' and '5 Keys' provides a great deal of clarity and focus. Many people find that their performance increases significantly by having this sharpened focus and definition. It allows them to sideline many of the distractions that might have been pulling them back and blunting their effectiveness.

However, the 5 Keys have another very powerful dimension. They can actually help you to become world class in your field. That sounds like an incredibly grandiose statement; one that over-promises and under-delivers. However, by using his 5 Keys, Chris Cook literally became the seventh fastest 100 meter breaststroke swimmer in history.

How?

The process is actually embarrassingly simple. I used the 5 Keys as the basis of a 'performance profile'; a simple tool that is used within sport psychology. We started by scoring Chris' ability in each of his 5 Keys on a scale, from zero to ten. A score of zero means that there is nothing good about this element at all. A score of ten means that it is perfect, flawless, and could not be improved in any way. Once we had a score for each area, we would find a strategy to increase that score during the coming weeks. We would also set a time scale (normally 4-6 weeks in Chris' case) and a way of assessing how successful we had been.

I did say it was alarmingly simple.

It is tempting to be dismissive at this point and think, "there's nothing new or earth shattering here". You might even feel a sense of anticlimax. The sub-title of this book is "sometimes the simplest ideas have the greatest impact". Often we become less effective when we over-complicate things. Although it may not be rocket-science, these are exactly the methods that I've used to help Chris, and many others, to become world class in their field.

The fact is, this process was incredibly effective because we used it consistently. We were constantly focused on improving the 5 most significant areas of Chris' performance. We honed as much of our focus as possible into these 5 areas because we knew that these had the greatest impact on his '2 Lengths'.

The Details

There were a couple of details that we consistently built into the process. For example, Chris and I often used a 4-6 week time-frame. This was not a random period of time. It worked for Chris because shorter time-scales suited his particular personality. Some people are able to focus for long periods of time. Others favour shorter bursts with regular reviews. Therefore we matched the time-frames to suit Chris.

Importantly, we would also spend time understanding what Chris' score actually meant. For example, if he scored his start as a 6/10, I would ask what a 6/10 looked like and how it differed from a 5/10 and a 7/10. This is an important part of the process for a couple of reasons. It gives some meaning to an arbitrary number. It also, crucially, helps us to know what a 7/10 looks like. If Chris' start is a 6/10, we need to know how we can make it better than a 6. It really helps if we have a clear understanding of what a 7 looks like and how it is different. I would often ask, 'How will we know when you're a 7? What will be different? How will a 7/10 look, sound, feel, think, act, talk?'

More recently, I have begun to understand that the score which a person provides is actually an average. In reality there is a range that exists around that average score. If I score myself as a 6/10, I'll have days when I might be an 8/10 and others when I am a 3/10. On some occasions the range could be significant (with a lot of variance between the best performance and worst), and in others it will be pretty tight. Understanding the range can also be very useful. It gives us a very easy way to improve our performance. If we're able to do those things that we do at the top end of the range more often, we will begin to change the score at the bottom end. If, in our example, we did those things that gave us an 8/10 all the time, we'd average 8/10 rather than 6/10. Essentially, by pulling the bottom end of the range up, we will increase our average performance. It's also likely that our very best days will also become better and therefore the top end of the range will also rise.

I find this system particularly effective when I'm working with people who are low in confidence. It is comforting for them to know that they can increase their performance by doing what they already do well. They simply need to do those things more often. They don't need to start doing new and unfamiliar things to improve their performance. There is no requirement for 'revolutionary' methods. In my experience, it is best to grow confidence on a solid base, by building on things that a person does know and can do.

Once we have asked these questions, and understood the answers, the strategy often writes itself.

Pinpoint the Priority
With the scores, ranges, an understanding of what all the numbers mean, and a strategy in place, we have some very tangible ways of improving our performance. The next question is, 'what do we do first?'

Having 5 Keys is a great way to start the process of honing your focus. However, we can't focus on 5 things all at the same time. So, within his 5 Keys, Chris and I would always look to identify those things that would have the greatest impact on his performance. We would tend to prioritise them and gave most attention to them. Of course, the priorities changed over time.

Sometimes we would focus on improving the area that received the lowest score, because we knew the importance of strengthening the weakest link in the chain. However, it was not always the case. Some areas of Chris' performance were simply more influential than others at times and therefore required the most attention.

As you go through the exercises yourself, you will notice that you can address several areas during any given period (whether that is 4-6 weeks or several months). However, it is always useful to understand the priorities and how each improvement impacts on your '2 Lengths'.

Metrics

Alongside our zero to ten scale, we had a number of metrics that helped us to track Chris' progress. Understanding how differently a 7/10 dive *felt*, to the 6/10, was crucial to Chris. The feel of the dive provided him with an internal, subjective, frame of reference. However, it was also vital that we had objective measurements which helped us to know that his 7/10 dive was actually quicker. There are a number of tools, in swimming, that help us to do that. The clever folk in the performance analysis team have high speed and underwater cameras. Using a frame-by-frame analysis, we could get a very accurate measure of the speed that Chris travelled during various stages of his start, both above and below the water's surface. The team could also digitise the footage to analyse joint angles, take off angles, entry angles and a whole host of other interesting things. Within all of this data, we identified a number of key metrics that we could use to measure elements of his start. The same, of course, applied to his other Keys. We could then use the zero to ten scale, and the metrics in tandem, to assess Chris' progress in the 5 most critical aspects of his performance.

Your Turn.

So, what are your 5 Keys?

How would you score your current performance on a scale of zero to ten?

What does a score one higher and one lower look like?

What is the range around each score? How good are you on your best days and worst days?

How can you increase your score by just one point in each area? What's the strategy?

What metrics can you use to track your progress?

When will you review and assess your progress?

Here's a very simple little table that I use to help the thought process and give it some structure. Feel free to use this one, or a similar version that works for you.

My 2 Lengths

Key	Score & Range	Top End & Bottom End	Strategy	Metrics / Evaluation
	... / 10 Range ...	Top End – Bottom End		

Here's an example of how it related to Chris' starts

Key	Score & Range	Top End & Bottom End	Strategy	Metrics / Evaluation
Fast Start	6 / 10 Range – 3-8	Top End – Strong body shape in the air. Bottom End – Too much movement in the air means I'm not streamlined underwater	More core stability work to help me maintain my shape in the air. Consistent pressure applied through both feet as I push on the blocks.	Track the angles from shoulders to knees and body rotation from the video analysis.

The Review

Personally, I believe that the most powerful phase of a 'plan – do – review' cycle is the review. Here's a little excerpt from an article that I wrote for Squash Player magazine (Issue 6, 2011, pages 28-29), which is available online at http://www.be-world-class.com/general/reviewing-your-mental-game-991 .

"In my sport psychology coaching I use a very simple formula; it's known as the 'plan – do – review'. To be honest, it's a bit of a misnomer. Its name suggests that the first stage of the cycle is to plan. In reality, the first stage is always the review because the review informs the plan. If we plan without a review, we do so blind-folded. How do we know what to work on? How do we know the essential things that we need to get right? How do we identify the things that are going to have a significant positive impact on our performance? All those questions are answered through our review.

In my opinion, the review is the most important element of the cycle. Sometimes awareness alone helps us to make positive changes to our game. Just being aware of what our mind and emotions are doing, helps us to take control of them. When working in a Premiership Rugby Union club a few years ago, we regularly filmed the players. Rather than filming the match, we would train the camera on specific individuals and track them for the entire game. On one occasion we followed a back-row forward. What we saw surprised us. Whenever this player went to ground in a tackle or a ruck, he would always be the last to get up. He then jogged over to the action and was the last to join it. Consequently, he was not particularly effective. The coaches decided to say nothing to the player, but simply sat him down to watch the footage. When we filmed him a month later, he was a far more effective player. It's amazing what we learn sometimes by watching ourselves.

Reviewing also helps us to start finding the resources that we need to improve our game. If we're struggling to hone our focus or to master our motivation, we might decide to type "hone focus in sport" or "master motivation in sport" into Google, or to check out some of the previous articles on these subjects in Squash Player! But that's not the only reason that the review is the key element in the plan – do – review. It also keeps the cycle together. If we only completed the 'plan' and the 'do', the cycle would end. By reviewing, we start the next cycle by informing the next planning stage. This simple formula helps us to continually learn and constantly improve."

As the excerpt suggests, the review stage pulls the cycle together and helps us to constantly improve. Right at the start of this section, I said that this very simple performance profiling system could potentially help you to become world class. I have spent many years studying world class performers (those who are literally in the top handful in the world in their chosen field). My second book, *How To Shine*, presents a culmination of my studies. When I look at a person's journey to becoming world-class, I notice that the 'secret' is often based on their ability to make constant improvements. Often these improvements are tiny. Sometimes the gains they make are almost invisibly small, which is why some people are unaware of them. However, by ensuring that their improvement is constant, the small gains accumulate and propel their performance.

Progress.

Are you better today than you were yesterday? What can you do today, to ensure that you're even better tomorrow? This remarkably simple thought process actually powers many people's journey to becoming world class. Their aim is not to become 'perfect'. We will never achieve perfection, because we're human. However, we can all achieve 'better'.

If I'm currently a 6/10, the logical next stage is to ask how I can become a 7/10. If I'd like to get closer to a 10/10, surely the next stop along the path is to move from 6 to 7. Often, moving from a 6 to a 7 is quite a challenging task in itself. Even that shift requires us to go from 6.0 to 6.1, then to 6.2 and so on.

Many people get caught in a trap because they try to jump from a 6/10 to a 10/10. Often it's easier to imagine what the 'perfect' model looks like. However, perfection is not easy to achieve. It's hard to understand the tangible changes that will turn a 6/10 into a 10/10. The pathway from 6/10 to 10/10 is less clear because we don't understand all of the steps that we need to make along the way.

A friend of mine talks of 'The Law of Persistence'. This law states that if you take consistent steps, in the direction that you wish to travel, there is only one outcome; eventually you will get there.

World class performers adopt a very similar mentality. They simply keep taking steps that will make them better today than they were yesterday, and better tomorrow than they are today. In doing so, they make constant progress.

"But I Haven't Got Time For This... I Have A Job To Do."
I spoke to an Executive about the importance of devoting time and effort to improving his 5 Keys. In response, he told me that he didn't have time for all of this because he had a job to do! Clearly he had not identified the 5 things that were most crucial to his 2 Lengths.

If your 5 Keys genuinely encapsulate the things that are most crucial to your performance, you will find it relatively easy to dedicate your time, energy and focus to constantly improving them.

6, 7, 8, 9, 4.
I have noticed a pattern developing whenever I work with athletes or executives for a prolonged period. They will typically start by scoring themselves fairly modestly on the performance profile. As a slight aside, I always find it fascinating that junior

athletes tend to score themselves reasonably highly (around the 8 and 9 out of 10 mark). World champions on the other hand, will often score themselves between 4 and 6 out of 10. As the athlete (or executive) makes progress, the score increases. If they started as a 5/10, they normally move through 6, 7 and 8. However, when they get to around an 8 or 9 out of 10, they start to see that they're not as close to that perfect 10 as they first thought. It's not unusual to find that they then start to revise their scoring and decide that it's more accurate to score themselves as a 4/10 again.

If you look at the scores and take them at face value, you'd ask why the person shot backwards from a 9/10 to a 4/10. The reality of course is that the 4/10 represents progress. All they have done is to realise that their proximity to 10 is not as close as they first imagined. I've noticed, when working with athletes for several years, that there can be many phases to this process (for example, when the work spans multiple Olympic cycles). Each time we go through the process we notice that the gains we make are smaller and the work required to achieve them is greater. In itself, this is an encouraging sign of progress. As we begin to approach an 'elite' or 'expert' level of performance, we begin to realise that the work required to make a 1 per cent gain is infinitely greater than it was when we were novices. We also start to notice that our focus turns to the tiny details.

Towards Mental Toughness

Mental Toughness is a term that has been commonplace in sport and sport psychology for many years. Interestingly, I have also seen it feature within business conversations during the last few years. Often terms like 'mental toughness' or 'mental strength' are used. Sometimes the component parts of mental toughness, such as resilience and tenacity are used. Whichever terms we use, many people now recognise that there are some challenges in the modern world, which require a 'tough mindset'.

Arguably, to be successful, we all need a healthy dose of mental toughness. I have seen first-hand evidence of its importance in my own work with world class athletes. In writing *How To Shine*, I also interviewed world class performers in a diverse range of disciplines outside of sport, to find out what differentiates them from their peers. It seems that mental toughness is also a key factor in the success of a twice Michelin starred chef, a world class mountaineer, a world barista champion, a record breaking polar explorer, the head of a world renowned science organisation and special-forces personnel. Mental toughness allows these people to push themselves and extend their limits. It enables them to thrive in adversity. Their mental toughness drives them to take on those challenges that their peers back away from. It allows them to constantly improve their performance by trying and failing! Perhaps more importantly, it also enables them to ask those uncomfortable, searching questions and find the difficult answers.

So, What Is Mental Toughness?

I believe that there are three component parts to mental toughness.

1. Resilience – the ability to thrive in adverse situations and 'bounce back' from set-backs.
2. Tenacity – the ability to run as hard as you can and keep on running, even when every fibre of your being wants to stop.
3. Composure – the ability to make great decisions and execute at a very high level, whatever is going on around you.

It is of course possible to see performers display some of these characteristics in isolation. Often athletes will show a great deal of grit and determination (tenacity), they'll overcome set-backs (resilience), but then lose out because they fail to display composure in those critical moments. I believe that true mental toughness is displayed when the three components are combined.

How Do We Develop Mental Toughness?

In my experience, mental toughness is not something that you can develop in isolation. It is actually a product of many different aspects of our 'mental game'. For example, it is very difficult to perform at your best in critical moments if you struggle to perform well consistently. Those who are able to consistently produce peak performances will stand a much greater chance of doing so 'under pressure'. Therefore, it is necessary to build the foundations first.

Most people perform well then they have three fundamental elements in place.

1. Focus
2. Confidence
3. Motivation

These three elements are inter-dependent and actually feed off of each other

Here's an excerpt from Chapter 2 of *Peak Performance Every Time* (p22-23), which explains this in more detail.

There is an interaction between the three components; they are dependent on each other. In reality they all impact on each other. If they were colours, they would merge together as a spectrum rather than being individual blobs on a page.

If we look at the relationship between the three more closely, it's actually possible to see how they affect each other.

When we have a simple, clear job, we have a very good chance of doing that job well (Baumeister & Showers, 1986; Donnelly & Ivancevich 1975). Obviously, we need to have the knowledge, skills, resources and desire to do it as well. But, having a simple, clear task initially gives us a massive advantage. Evidence for this concept comes from a variety of sources. Researchers in management settings have identified that both task clarity (Lindsley, Brass & Thomas, 1995) and role clarity (Bray & Brawley, 2002a, 2002b) have a significant impact on performance.

When we understand the job, we're able to do it well. When we do the job well, we normally get a sense of satisfaction and fulfilment. Typically, as human beings, we like exhibiting mastery and we like to be successful in the things we do. So, when we perform well at something, we tend to want to do it again (Kloosterman, 1988). Psychologists, such as Albert Bandura (1997) have identified strong links between mastery, confidence, achievement and motivation.

These links sets up our positive spiral.

When I'm *focused* on a simple, clear job I give myself the best chance of being successful.

When I have done the job well I become *confident* and enjoy doing it.

When I am confident in doing something, I am *motivated* to do it again.

Our 2 Lengths gives us this initial point of focus. Once we have the focus, we're likely to do the job well. When we focus on the processes, we normally perform close to our best. Our 2 Lengths keeps the job simple and clear. It allows us to see the job for what it really is. Chris' job was to swim 2 lengths as fast as he could, not to beat the world record holder. This simple, clear focus therefore helps us to feel confident in our ability to do the job well.

Controlling Confidence

What do you think most people's confidence is under-pinned by? Often the answer is "results". However, that's not a strong position to be in. If your confidence is reliant upon winning or losing, it is going to be pretty fragile. Winning and losing is something you cannot directly control. There are a huge number of factors that dictate the result in a sporting contest. For example, although you have a certain degree of influence, you can't control the referee. I've seen referees have an enormous impact on results. Do you really want refereeing decisions to underpin your confidence?

What other factors underpin confidence? To be honest, there are potentially hundreds. Common factors include feedback, which could come from coaches, managers, peers or parents. I worked with a professional footballer (soccer player) a few years ago who was lacking confidence. We chatted about what influenced his confidence. It emerged that the manager had the biggest influence, followed by other players, the crowd, his Dad and even the newspaper report. When we looked at it objectively, the chances are that the manager's feedback was not going to be completely reliable. The manager will be watching 20+ players on the field and not really focusing on him. If they win, the manager is likely to be happy with him. If they lose he won't. That also goes for the other players, the crowd and the newspaper. As we chatted, it became apparent that the players' own views counted for very little. Ironically, of course, the player himself was in the best position to review his game and probably had the most accurate feedback. He'd seen and felt his performance from inside his body.

This example shows that controlling confidence often starts with how we control feedback. Our footballer started to control his confidence when he started to honestly and objectively evaluate his own performances. It sounds pretty simple and straight forward, but let's take a look at that in more detail. Firstly, he needs to be honest. If he has had a poor game, he needs to be honest about it. Equally, if he's played really well, he needs to be honest rather than modest. Secondly, he needs to be objective. This means that he can use his own evaluation and then integrate feedback from others. The aim is not to be arrogant and ignore the feedback of others. The aim is to use the benefit of both.

Finally, our player needs to evaluate. Most players don't evaluate, they judge. Normally the judgement is emotionally charged and contains little in the way of useful information. How many times have you described your performance as "good", "ok" or "****". None of those have any value. When I work with athletes I start by asking them to rate their performance on a scale of 0-10. It's never going to be a zero. There will always be something in it that was positive. Equally, it's very rare that a performance would be a 'perfect' (flawless) 10. Whatever you score, there will always be two elements to your score. What did you do well (which stopped you from scoring 0)? What can you improve (which stopped you from scoring 10)? Knowing these two things will help you ensure that your next performance is better than this one.

But what happens if I scored a 2? Surely I'm not going to be confident going into the next game.

Here are a few ideas from *How To Shine* (page 91)

Mistakes Provide Confidence.

I have seen very successful athletes using their mistakes to increase their confidence (that's right, *increase* their confidence). Imagine two athletes, who both have disappointing performances. The first athlete feels upset and gets disheartened, so they try to forget the performance. They go back into training and do the same things they did before. The second athlete also feels upset, but decides to go through the uncomfortable task of reviewing the performance in detail. They identify the things that went wrong and work hard on them in training. A couple of weeks later, they can see tangible improvements in those areas of their game. The second athlete is not making the same mistakes now. Who do you think will go into their next competition feeling more confident?

There is a very simple formula, which you can use to create confidence. Build on what you can do! In the spring I sat down with a junior international archer. I asked why she looked troubled. She told me she was dreading school, particularly Business Studies. I challenged her to tell me five questions that she would love to see on the exam paper because she knew the answers. After a little grouching and muttering she agreed. Next day she said she had seven questions. "Great" I said, "your job now is to research five more questions so that you know them inside out. Once you know these, you'll have 12". I then asked her how confident she would feel if she had 150 questions that she'd love to see on the exam paper, because she knew the answers. Of course, she'd feel confident. So, the formula is simple. Once you've got 12, research another five, then another five until you have enough to feel truly confident.

This very simple system shows that we can take control of our confidence when we honestly and objectively evaluate our performance against our 5 Keys. How good was our performance today on a zero to ten scale? What can we do to improve it? If we genuinely work on these areas of our game, we are much more likely to go into our next performance more confident.

Accountability.

When researching *How To Shine*, I became aware that taking responsibility and accountability, is central to mental toughness. In fact, characteristics such as discipline, accountability and professionalism underpin mental toughness. Many managers will recognise this in their people. The question is; how do you foster accountability?

The truth is, it's very difficult to hold someone accountable if they're not sure what they're being held accountable for. It sounds obvious, I know, but often it is a lack of clarity that prevents people from taking accountability. I first came to realise how the 2 Lengths impacts on accountability when working in professional soccer in the UK. The manager of the team was getting increasingly frustrated because his players would not take accountability for their performances. The team were losing, performing poorly and slipping down the league table. Often the manager would march into the dressing room after the game and ask why no-one on the field took responsibility or accountability for their own performance. As they left the stadium, I asked one of the players how he felt he'd played. His answer was, "I think I did okay. I wasn't great, made a couple of mistakes, but I did my job". At training, the following day, I asked the manager how he felt the player had performed. The manager's answer was, "he just didn't do his job". This simple example highlights the core of the issue. The player's view of his job was not the same as the manager's view. They didn't share the same view of this player's 2 Lengths of the Pool.

Of course, this player was one of a squad of around 18 regular first team players. The issue was not unique to him; it applied equally to the other 17 players as well. When we looked a little deeper, we found that the 'job' that had been outlined was simply too vague. Although some of the same words were used, the players and the management had very different views on what they meant and what was actually expected. Sometimes the 'job' would be defined by outcomes, such as 'score goals'. However, the outcomes were not entirely under the player's control. A player could play as well as possible but simply not score a goal because he didn't get good service from his team mates. Equally, he may score the goal but have the goal disallowed because of a poor refereeing decision, or have his shots saved by the opposing goal-keeper.

As I started working with the squad, I asked each of the players to outline their 2 Lengths and 5 Keys. We worked hard to make sure that they were as specific and clear as possible, so that we could eradicate any ambiguity. I also challenged the manager and the coaching staff to do the same. At the end of the exercise we discovered that there were a huge variety of differing views. During the following few weeks we refined each player's 2 Lengths and 5 Keys, and made sure that everyone (the player, manager, coaches and team-mates) all had the same understanding of each player's job. We also spent time looking at footage from the previous few games so that we could help the players, management and coaching team to develop a common view of the standards expected. I asked everyone to score the performance for a number of specific incidents during the game. We looked at all of the scores and discussed the differences of opinion. We identified ways of evaluating the performance using both 'judgement' and quantifiable data. This process helped the group to have a shared understanding of their jobs, individually and collectively, and a common view of the standard expected.

As a result of the exercise, the manager was able to hold players accountable for delivering their 2 Lengths and 5 Keys. The players knew that it was their responsibility to deliver their 2 Lengths. Once the players and management had a shared view, the manager was able to say, "It is your responsibility to deliver your 2 Lengths on match day. We will help you and support you as much as possible, but it's your responsibility". These simple principles lead to a significant change in the behaviour of the squad. We noticed that the players would take a much more proactive approach in training. Rather than waiting for the coaching staff to dictate the work, players would start asking for help to develop the areas of their game that they needed to improve. There was a recognition that the 'hard work' needed to be done between the games and not just on match day. Before we conducted this exercise many players would say, "I did my best on the field". Some of them would come off of the field physically exhausted after a game, having given everything they could. However, in truth, they were exhausted because they had not invested enough effort in the physical fitness work during the week. Therefore, although they worked as hard as they could in each game, their capacity on match day was not as great as it could have been. This was also true for their skills and tactical awareness. In order to turn around their results on the field, each player was challenged to be better tomorrow than they are today... and better today than they were yesterday.

For more details on this case study, read Chapter 11 of *Peak Performance Every Time*.

Case Study

To help understand how all of this works in practice, I thought it would be helpful to provide a case study. This particular example is taken from work that I did with the Law Firm in the UK. It was the first time I'd applied the '2 Lengths' principles to a larger organisation (one with over 100 people). It highlights some of the challenges that we encountered, gives an insight into what we did and how we did it.

First Stage.

I was approached initially by the HR Director of the firm. She had seen me present at a Conference a few weeks previously and asked whether I could do some one-to-one Executive Coaching with the Managing Partner of the firm. The HR Director felt that he was suffering from "too much to do, and too little time to do it, syndrome". So, at the beginning of the Executive Coaching programme, we established the 2 Lengths and 5 Keys for the Managing Partner. Initially it was a bit of a culture shock because it required him to relinquish control of things that were not actually part of his 5 Keys, but that he'd habitually involved himself in. As the Managing Partner began to follow his 2 Lengths and 5 Keys, he noticed that he became far more effective. He created space, which he could use for the genuinely important elements of his role, such as 'strategic thinking time'. Of course, having more time presents a challenge in itself. There is a temptation that having 'spare' time feels uncomfortable. Many executives actually feel guilty if they are not working at 100 miles per hour for 20 hours a day. There seems to be a collective expectation in business that everyone should work harder, be busier and do more hours; not less. Once he'd got his head around all of this, the Managing Partner was able to ensure that he dedicated his time to his 2 Lengths and 5 Keys, and allowed other people to get on with their own jobs.

The Senior Team.

After a little while, the Managing Partner also asked me to work with a number of his senior management team. He had started to realise that he was only one person within the business, and that there were others who would also become more effective if they knew their 2 Lengths and 5 Keys. As I worked with the other members of the team it became apparent that they did not all share the same view of the firm's 2 Lengths of the Pool. Although the views were not radically different, each person had their own perspective. It raised an interesting question. If we asked all 32 of the Equity Partners and Board Members to propose a '2 Lengths' for the firm, how many different answers would we get?

We decided to pull all of the senior management team together for an away day to explore this question. It was a fascinating exercise. We found that there were quite a diverse set of views. We spent a considerable amount of time debating whether the word 'profitable' should be included in their 2 Lengths. A law firm is a commercial business. However, there were several members of the team that didn't feel that profitability should be included. It raised an important question that they needed to resolve. In addition, the team were able to distil exactly what they did as a business and how they did it. They were therefore able to identify their collective priorities and make sure that they could focus the entire firm on delivering them.

Following the away day, the senior partners spent an additional three to four weeks discussing and agreeing their 2 Lengths and 5 Keys. This period of time allowed everyone to resolve those outstanding issues and ensure that the senior management team were all on 'the same page'. The team were also able to stress test their 2 Lengths and 5 Keys, to ensure that they were robust.

The Cascade.

Once we were happy that there was a collective agreement, the team started to look at their own departments 2 Lengths and 5 Keys. This is the first stage of the process by which we could 'cascade' the approach throughout the whole firm. Each member of the senior management team engaged their department to identify the 2 Lengths and 5 Keys for the group. When each department was happy that they had a clear focus, which was aligned with that of the firm as a whole, we reviewed the 2 Lengths and 5 Keys for all of the departments together.

This helped us to understand whether there were any holes or overlaps, and also identify the lines of inter-dependency that existed. It took a few weeks to iron these out, but it was a very worthwhile process. Looking back, I think that this stage alone had a really positive impact in helping the departments and senior managers to 'gel' as a team.

With the all of the departments aligned to the firm, we could then roll the programme out to the rest of the business. To help smooth the process we decided to take a burden off of the managers. Rather than asking them to explain the '2 Lengths of the Pool' concept to their teams, we got everyone together and delivered a session to the entire firm. This helps to avoid the 'Chinese whispers' (which could distort the message). The session was opened by the Managing Partner, who described the process so far, the rationale and the positive outcomes that they'd experienced. Chris Cook and I gave some background behind the '2 Lengths' mind-set, how we'd stumbled upon it and the effect that it had on Chris' performance. The session was filmed and uploaded to the firm's intranet. The collective 2 Lengths and 5 Keys were printed onto mouse mats and appeared in other prominent places throughout the business. Each person within the business was challenged to identify their own 2 Lengths and 5 Keys, understand how it complemented the rest of their team, aligned to their department and to the firm as a whole.

2 Lengths Embedded.

As you can imagine, this process didn't happen overnight. Some people drove it more than others. There were members of the firm who just 'got it'. Some departments adopted it quickly and completely. Others took longer, picking up little bits at first and then adopting more of the principles as they went along. To help the firm ensure that the 2 Lengths lived and breathed, we began to embed it within the HR systems and processes.

A few years previously, I had worked in an English First Class County Cricket Club. The ECB (England & Wales Cricket Board) noted that there was a disparity between the HR processes surrounding the playing staff and the processes that applied to the rest of the staff at the club (i.e. management, coaching, medical, marketing, finance, ground staff, etc). All of the non-playing staff had regular formal appraisals. However, the players hadn't ever been subjected to the same process. Therefore, we were challenged to build an 'appraisal' and performance management system around the players. Our solution was to use the 2 Lengths and 5 Keys as the structure for our performance management with the players.

The principles were very simple. Each player had a personal 2 Lengths and 5 Keys, and a performance profile score which had been agreed with the coaching staff. These were processes, not outcomes. We worked hard to ensure that there was a fair and objective way of assessing their performance in each area. The players also had targets for each of their 5

Keys and strategies to increase their performance. If players exceeded the targets that were agreed, they received bonuses. If they fell short, we would start to look at the reasons why. In some cases players required some support from the club, such as sport science, sports medicine or coaching support. In other cases, the players needed to become more professional; prepare themselves better for matches and practice sessions, train harder or focus more on their game.

In order to help the 2 Lengths and 5 Keys 'live and breathe' in the Law Firm, we applied exactly the same system. The appraisal system focused on reviewing each person's performance against their 2 Lengths and 5 Keys. Of course, staff, management and HR needed to have a clear and shared understanding of how to evaluate progress and performance in each area. If a member of staff exceeded their targets, they were rewarded. If they fell short, the firm started to look for the reasons and potential solutions. Some team members needed to attend courses for further training, some required coaching, others received a 'kick up the backside' (not literally of course!).

The firm found that embedding the 2 Lengths and 5 Keys within the appraisal system allowed it to become a part of their everyday operation. Aligning the 2 Lengths and 5 Keys with the incentive structure also ensured that the team were actively engaged and focused on their delivery. The result is that each member of the team starts to focus their time, energy, effort and resource onto those things that have the greatest impact.

Everyone becomes more effective. The distractions disappear into the background, rather than consuming the team's attention. As each individual performs better, the team as a whole benefits many times over. Managers also reported that their lives became easier when their people were focused, confident, motivated and took accountability for their performance. Instead of spending considerable time tied up 'fire-fighting' and dealing with 'management issues', they were able to dedicate more time and energy to propelling the team forwards.

Simple Does Not Always Mean Easy.

Finding your 2 Lengths and 5 Keys helps to simplify and clarify. However, simple does not necessarily mean easy. Chris Cook found that simplifying his job created challenges of its own. In fact he said, at the Be World Class Conference 2011, "The biggest challenge was buying into simplifying it".

The first challenge, for Chris, was to wrestle with his own ego. When I first proposed that Chris' job was simply to swim 2 lengths of a pool as fast as he could, he felt gutted. He described feeling as if I'd struck an acupuncture point and that I'd undermined his job. As Chris later recognised, it was his ego that felt bruised, not his 'true self'.

The second challenge that Chris and his coach faced, was to take the leap of faith. Chris understood that by dedicating himself to his '2 Lengths', he was going against the grain. It meant stepping away from those things that he'd always done. He would leave the familiar territory and start a journey into the unknown. He abandoned the conventions by which everyone else worked. He no longer subscribed to swimming 60,000+ meters per week. Chris knew very well that that there were a lot of swimmers in the world who had become very successful by following the conventional route, and yet he was stepping away from it. Most of his competitors were over-complicating their performances and doing very well. The 'traditional' and 'conventional' methods had also helped Chris rise from the junior ranks to become an international. Therefore, he was not choosing to abandon methods that failed. He was choosing to abandon methods that worked, in order to find some that worked even more effectively for him.

As Chris introduced the '2 Lengths' concept to his support team (his physiotherapist, strength & conditioning coach, physiologist, etc), we began to encounter the third challenge. Some of the team didn't want to embrace simplicity because they liked complexity. It placed Chris in quite an awkward position. He is the kind of guy who likes to be liked. In his own words, he's a people pleaser. In essence, he was delivering a message that some of the team were just not keen on. The physiologist on the team provided the greatest resistance. He loved data, graphs and numbers... and lots of them! He enjoyed the complexity and revelled in it. His natural instinct was to expand, rather than refine. Therefore, he found it tough to buy into a drive towards simplicity.

As the team began to live the '2 Lengths' concept, we saw the real power that comes with simplicity and clarity. Ambiguity often provides a hiding place for people; a place where 'fudged' answers and half-baked solutions can survive. Clarity removes ambiguity and therefore takes away that hiding place. The clarity enabled us, as a team, to ask direct questions of each other. We would ask how new ideas or methods actually contributed to the 2 Lengths. It took us all outside of our comfort zone. We could not say, "Because that's the way we've always done it". We needed to justify our answers. If we were not fully convinced by the answers, we would do more work on the idea before bringing it back. We had some very well defined criteria from which to work and clear points of reference. The simplicity and clarity that we created therefore demanded more from us. The questions were easier but the answers were harder. We needed to think about them in more detail, become more diligent and come up with answers that were more complete.

It seems that simplicity and clarity are not for the faint hearted.

Summary

In the spirit of keeping things simple, here is a very straight forward summary of this book.

- What is your '2 Lengths'? What's your job, in the simplest possible terms?

- What are the 5 Key things that you need to do, in order to deliver your '2 Lengths'?

- How would you score your ability to deliver these 5 Keys, on a scale of 0-10?

- How can you increase your scores by just 1 point? What's your strategy?

- How will you assess and review your progress?

- How can you align your team to ensure that everyone's '2 Lengths' contributes completely to the '2 Lengths' of the team?

I did say that it was all alarmingly simple.

What's Next?

You now have the basic tools. You can find your own 2 Lengths and 5 Keys. You may also feel confident in helping other people to find theirs. In addition to the information in this book, you'll also find that *Peak Performance Every Time* and *How To Shine* are valuable resources.

What's Next?

If you have found this short book valuable, and would like to take more steps towards becoming world class, why not **become a member of Be World Class**, by registering at www.be-world-class.com.

Membership of Be World Class is ideal for entrepreneurs, athletes, business executives, sports coaches & sport psychologists, business coaches, senior business leaders (CEOs and MDs), athletic directors and performance directors.

Members receive a vast array of tools and resources that focus on

- Maximising personal performance
- How to work towards becoming world class in your field

- How to take on 'impossible' challenges
- World class leadership
- How to develop world class teams

And

- How to build world class organisations

FREE BONUS MATERIAL

As a 'thank you' for reading this book, I'd like to offer you some exclusive free bonus materials. Simply go to www.be-world-class.com/bonus and register your details. You'll find a wealth of free information, including interviews with double Olympian, Chris Cook, podcasts, articles, webinars and videos.

If you have questions, or would like to join in discussions on world class performance, feel free to join the 'be world class' LinkedIn group (http://www.linkedin.com/groups/be-world-class-3885888) and follow @worldclasssimon on Twitter.

Although it is alarmingly simple, the '2 Lengths' concept has made an incredible difference to the performance, and lives, of many people and organisations. Chris Cook describes it as 'genuinely life changing'. Chris, and many other ordinary people, found that this simple concept propelled them towards becoming world class.

Could this very simple idea change your life too?

Bibliography and Useful Links

Bandura, A. (1997) *Self-efficacy: The exercise of control*, New York: Worth Publishers.

Baumeister, R.F. and Showers, C.J. (1986) 'A review of paradoxical performance effects: Choking under pressure in sports and mental tests', *European Journal of Social Psychology*, 16(4), 361-383.

Bray, S.R. and Brawley, L.R. (2002a) 'Role Efficacy, Role Clarity and Role Performance Effectiveness', *Small Group Research*, 33(2), 233-253

Bray, S.R. and Brawley, L.R. (2002b) 'Efficacy for Independent Role Functions: Evidence from the Sport Domain, *Small Group Research*, 33(6), 644-666.

Donnelly, J.H. and Ivancevich, J.M. (1975) 'Role Clarity and the Salesman', *Journal of Marketing*, 39(1), 71-74.

Hartley, S. R. (2007) 'Are You Thinking What Your Athlete Is Thinking?', *Coaching Edge*, 8, 20-21.

Hartley, S.R. (2010a) 'Controlling Your Confidence', *Squash Player*, 38(1), 15.

Hartley, S.R. (2010b) 'No Such Thing As Pressure', *Squash Player*, 38(2), 19.

Hartley, S.R. (2010c) 'Real Goals', *Squash Player*, 38(3), 17.

Hartley, S.R. (2010d) 'Motivation: The Driving Force', *Squash Player*, 38(4), 22.

Hartley, S.R. (2010e) 'Learn From Everything', *Squash Player*, 38(6), 24.

Hartley, S.R. (2010f) 'Athletic Focus & Sport Psychology: Key To Peak Performance', *Podium Sports Journal*, December 2010. Available Online. HTTP. < http://www.podiumsportsjournal.com/2010/12/09/athletic-focus-sport-psychology-key-to-peak-performance/> (accessed 21st December 2010).

Hartley, S.R. (2010g) 'Momentum Shifts in Sport: Value the Psychology Behind Them', *Podium Sports Journal*, December 2010. Available Online. HTTP. < http://www.podiumsportsjournal.com/2010/12/22/momentum-shifts-in-sports-value-the-psychology-behind-them/> (accessed 4th April 2011)

Hartley, S.R. (2011a) 'Maintaining Momentum', *Squash Player*, 39(2), 28-29.

Hartley, S.R. (2011b) *Peak Performance Every Time*, London: Routledge.

Hartley, S.R. (2012a) *How To Shine; Insights into unlocking your potential from proven winners*, Chichester: Capstone.

Hartley, S.R. (2012b) 'Pressure; Fantasy or Reality', *Leaders In Performance*, 2nd May 2012. Available Online. HTTP. < http://www.leadersinperformance.com/the-leader/simon-hartley-pressure-fantasy-or-reality/> (accessed 3rd January 2013).

Kloosterman, P. (1988) 'Self Confidence and Motivation in Mathematics', *Journal of Educational Psychology*, 80(3), 345-351.

Lindsley, D.H., Brass, D.J. and Thomas, J.B. (1995) 'Efficacy-Performance Spirals: A Multilevel Perspective', *Academy of Management Review*, 20(3), 645-678.

About Simon Hartley

Simon Hartley is globally respected sport psychology consultant and performance coach. He helps athletes and business people throughout the world to get their mental game right. During the last 17 years, he has worked with gold medalists, world record holders, world champions, top 5 world ranked professional athletes and championship winning teams.

Simon has worked at the highest level of sport, including spells in Premiership football, Premiership rugby union, First Class County Cricket, Super League, golf, tennis, motor sport and with Great British Olympians.

Since 2005, Simon has also applied the principles of sport psychology to business, education, healthcare and the charity sector. This has included projects with some of the world's leading corporations and foremost executives.

Recently, Simon has also become a respected author and professional speaker.

His first book, *Peak Performance Every Time*, was published by Routledge in 2011. He followed this with his second, *How To Shine*, which was published by Capstone in 2012. Simon has also delivered three Be World Class Conferences, which are available online at www.beworldclass.tv

Made in the USA
San Bernardino, CA
23 November 2015